D1530949

The Mountain/West Poetry Series
Stephanie G'Schwind, Donald Revell, Kazim Ali,
Dan Beachy-Quick & Camille T. Dungy, series editors

We Are Starved, by Joshua Kryah
The City She Was, by Carmen Giménez Smith
Upper Level Disturbances, by Kevin Goodan
The Two Standards, by Heather Winterer
Blue Heron, by Elizabeth Robinson
Hungry Moon, by Henrietta Goodman
The Logan Notebooks, by Rebecca Lindenberg
Songs, by Derek Henderson
The Verging Cities, by Natalie Scenters-Zapico
A Lamp Brighter than Foxfire, by Andrew S. Nicholson
House of Sugar, House of Stone, by Emily Pérez
&luckier, by Christopher J Johnson
Escape Velocity, by Bonnie Arning
We Remain Traditional, by Sylvia Chan
The Lapidary's Nosegay, by Lara Candland
Furthest Ecology, by Adam Fagin
The Minuses, by Jami Macarty
Dears, Beloveds, by Kevin Phan

DEARS, BELOVEDS

DEARS, BELOVEDS

poems

KEVIN PHAN

The Center for Literary Publishing
Colorado State University

For information about permission to reproduce
selections from this book, write to:
The Center for Literary Publishing
attn: Permissions
9105 Campus Delivery
Colorado State University
Fort Collins, Colorado 80523-9105.

Printed in the United States of America.

Library of Congress Cataloging-in-Publication Data

Names: Phan, Kevin, 1979- author.
Title: Dears, beloveds : poems / Kevin Phan.
Other titles: Mountain west poetry series.
Description: Fort Collins, Colorado :
The Center for Literary Publishing, Colorado State University, [2020]
| Series: The Mountain west poetry series
Identifiers: LCCN 2020035657 (print) | LCCN 2020035658 (ebook) |
ISBN 9781885635754 (paperback) | ISBN 9781885635761 (ebook)
Subjects: LCSH: Grief--Poetry. | LCGFT: Poetry.
Classification: LCC PS3616.H376 D43 2020 (print) | LCC PS3616.
H376 (ebook) | DDC 811/.6--dc23
LC record available at https://lccn.loc.gov/2020035657
LC ebook record available at https://lccn.loc.gov/2020035658

The paper used in this book meets the minimum requirements of the
American National Standard for Information Sciences-Permanence of
Paper for Printed Library Materials, ANSI Z39.48-1984.

Publication of this book was made possible by a grant
from the National Endowment for the Arts.

ART WORKS.

National
Endowment
for the Arts
arts.gov

It will be a pity if you
don't know what a mango is.
                    —Thich Nhat Hanh

Your absence has gone through me
Like thread through a needle.
Everything I do is stitched with its color.
                    —W. S. Merwin

Child. We are done for
in the most remarkable ways.
                    —Brigit Pegeen Kelly

Contents

DEARS, BELOVEDS

[Outside the snapdragons, cords of light]

*

Outside the snapdragons, cords of light. Today's easy as weeds & winds & early. Green hills shift green. Cardinals peck at feeders—our air salted with seeds. A power line across the road blows blue bolts. Crickets generate crickets in the grass. We are made & remade together. An ant circles the sugar cube. Our shadow's a blown sail running blue over cracked tiles. Tin stars burst bold from the fridge—blue applause. Cool glistening pours from the tap, even on the edges. Time, in balanced soil, grows inside the snapdragons. In the sizzling cast iron, a membrane slit, a sunny side runs yellow down the pan. If the weatherman ain't spitting lies, the rain falls freely where you live, too! A red wire, a live red wire, a temperature.

[Floating sheep turn to wonder]

*

Floating sheep turn to wonder. Silver pots throw a blue shadow across the range. We carry this the length of our lives. Tall stones lining the garden flower at once. Morning winds, columbines crash—the turf applauds. 2 reeling petal-whorls gleam, then break. Happy birthday, oak—perfect in another ring. Branch shadows fall across the window in perfect accident without weight. Orange sponge, a million suds to a squeeze, know your water. Add a few phrases to the sunrise & pinks pop. Fossils beneath the garden are a choir underground. Garlic, ginger & mangoes hang in tiers in a cradle of red wire. That paw at the door is an aluminum fever. Everything the worms do for the hills is in secret & enough. Corolla of petals, shift your atoms toward the bright.

[I pass through the mental hospital]

*

I pass through the mental hospital. What thin ghosts. Each howl a rupture we can't smooth in. *They don't know they don't know. They don't know they don't know. Mother, what can't each of them know?* Thrashing seems crazy. My brothers, my sisters, tender & lost. Hearts changing colors in a room of changing hearts. *All rise!* Sometimes, beings who loved & tortured & mothered me in former lives respond to my prayers, egging me on. Compassion for my family, born into serial pain—for any living being forced to crush it on the daily just to chafe & blister against vast walls. Sometimes existing in wildly diminished states. Kinship of neon lights & Milk Moon mothers. *May I help all beings, in all worlds, in all ways.* Hearts drip fire. Tell me, sweet pal, if the kettle starts boiling.

[To witness a selkie, owl-grandmother, grief]

*

To witness a selkie, owl-grandmother, grief a bully-knee zeroing out my lungs. Rib cage shattered by flex. Short rhymes of greener weather. *Can we be brought into being without bringing life to blows?* Stuff I love & fear, through sentences, float. (Pointillism like impacts of cancer kisses.) The Encyclopedia of *I-Can't-Believe-My-Eyes,* longer each day. Mother's head snapping wild on the stem. A blues full of cruel. Elbow deep in suds, washing wounds. "Why don't you *fucking* die already," said father, breeding knives. Cried mom, "meanest thing anybody's ever said," floating down herself into herself, to nowhere living. I fed her mango smoothies, for loud pains. Our pollution story is not *so* uncommon. Sometimes, living's simply the botched fur coat we shed.

[For each today, I'll let my soul-force lead]

*

For each today, I'll let my soul-force lead. Cherry trees living deep in our garden, robed in evanescent bees. Fireflies melt luminescence into our faces. Emissaries from a realm more beautiful than our own. In meditation, the instruction comes—"gather every funk & sorrow into one. Place your fear-botched heart in the cradle of loving-kindness." *Why must being end? Can we be mended as we shatter? Won't you tell me, now, if this will be a long life?* Imaginary beasts float to my skin's translucent surface from within, knives for teeth, lusting MEAT. Cancer making cancer of cancer, cruel replication machines all the way down. *Quarrelsome mind, hush up!* Our neighborhood church grows fat with gospel—sour longing hearts—"yes lord, yes lord, yes lord, bring-a-me home."

[Eternal waves quarrel at the bottom of a well full of blueness]

*

Eternal waves quarrel at the bottom of a well full of blueness. (My heart.) Afterlife of red, eyeless ghosts. Unmoored, unstrung—each a declassified ancestor. *Who doesn't go home?* We who trance at the blast. We who skylight our skullcaps to bleed in this lushness. Cells within the rivers we are shaped by, somehow shaping. Invisibility's gamut whelms our hearts. Pleats of fractal distance. "Build the wall." (Space is champagne glittering in every gill.) *Won't you strap me back on time's wheel & teach me to sing?* The song of clueless children collaging lavender, saving a family of doomed lambs from the one-armed butcher. (Hearts full of hours.) I am a child again. Stormy purple thunders collapsing down my neck. Master says, "everything's overlapping presences." "EV-REE-THING!" he doubles down. *How will I protect my sacred loneliness now?*

[Sweet jumping Jesus, bright flocks of rain!]

*   .

Sweet jumping Jesus, bright flocks of rain! Waves sharp as sticks, chewing our earth to soft. Dandelions, seeds on wings. It's hard to set down roots in running water. Compassion allows us to widen from within. Soon, all were singing, cicadas & trailer folk. All these generations. Brown boys & brown girls, mantling scaffolds, self-deporting, laughing at field-rotting vegetables no one will touch. The underground railroad lived just down the street. (We feel solemn gratitude for its grace.) In Buddhist scripture, Avalokiteshvara reaches w/1,000 arms & hands into the pits of suffering to soften human bruises—blue waves closing 'round bowls of fetid fire. I pray alone for everyone, wishing enlightenment from suffering as life's peak gift, nourishing the courage to save myself for last. & Even with Buddha as pilot, flying gives me the shakes. Conditionless friendship, no strings, for the love of, float on.

[Beneath dark purples, new life jockeying through the cracks]

*

Beneath dark purples, new life jockeying through the cracks. "It's a beautiful day in the neighborhood . . . Won't you be my neighbor?" Sex moans & rabbit skulls. "Build the wall!" Harmonic sighs of ocean oscillations. (Percussive distance.) Immigrant offspring, my family. An American version of disembodied, we failed to root. Pineapples dream they eat an ice cream sandwich. In the mammogram, a black-star fist. Love's only as real as the ancestors passing through us. Outside, the sky does miraculous things to the trees. I never wanted my mother's living much further from my own. Imagine surrender. Imagine Kevin self-bleaching his soul just to smooth in. Flattened with a baking pin. Zeroed down to flour. Of course it hurt, still hurts. *Us vs. them, there vs. here,* a contiguity of angles to unlearn.

[What brought us from the ocean into diamond Buddhafields?]

*

What brought us from the ocean into diamond Buddhafields? Is enlightenment *just* another myth? Noam Chomsky, precisely scripting our dissent. We're stuck here waiting, wanting to be wanted back, toddling through space, ducking greasy slumlords, planting kisses & bleeding the drugs in. This, my heart, a punch of ancient honey. Each gust of wind collapses through my fingers. (Mouth full of mango, chewing the world past soft.) I press my cheek against the rainy glass, thinking (once more) of Berryman. "The artist is extremely lucky who is presented with the worst possible ordeal which will not actually kill him," he famously professed. Freud's *death drive*. An appeal *so* real. My own longing for end points in the rearview for now. From a falling speck of dust, a falling shadow. Our mouths, tiny circles of awe. It's hard to set down roots in running water.

[Kombucha & skincare]

*

Kombucha & skincare. Ointment & rice paper. Oil
changes, jasmine dreams, sun salutations. I pray alone.
For everyone. Loving intentions float up & through my
living kitchen. Feelings, big as barns, glide toward the
sun. Lost in bright confusions, bone cancer at the center—
"she loved us once." *Does god care for shipwrecked
vessels, tending to the sick as their bodies, one by one,
disintegrate beyond trembles?* A feel-good comedy,
except *some* people, or flesh approaching compost.
"May all beings reach enlightenment, quickly." (All the
bats of the universe geolocate inside my prison cell.)
*Precious human birth—life I plan to taste just once—
what's one pure act I've done?* A lyric running down my
godless honey scraps. What a lesson. Something about
how hunger swells us close to education.

[Here's the church, here's the steeple]

*

Here's the church, here's the steeple & here's the hospital, full of marked people. Somehow, the patient who choked down the raw honey sun spent the evening tucking bloody lions into bed. We live with no true sense of how our worlds became. & To bear witness is to be alive within our cuts. I witnessed many occasions of it. Hospice nurses swaddled in goose down, chain smoking Marlboros behind blue snows. Many occasions of it. Haloes of IV tubing cocooning naked bodies in soft. Many occasions of it. Scars reshaped into beauty marks by an exclusive, well-placed kiss. Margins increase. Red wine matures below a cork. Try (if you can manage it) to love each hour with your whole heart. Between snapdragons & the big bang, this grave of washed-out stars.

[I walk past the mental hospital]

*

I walk past the mental hospital. Mother lived there
once—mid-20s—her spectrum fractured past tears.
Map corrupted & the roads erased. Friendliness
without conditions toward all beings. Every animal in
every kingdom. Your heart in my heart. *Tell me where
it hurts.* According to Thy wills, lords within, these
walls of storms. Root beer floats & wheelchair-bound
happy (final) birthday. Cubbies took the World Series—
applause sewn in. Caramel cheesecake & high fives all
around! "If it's not one thing, it's another"—mother
sank—"I'll be dead soon." How like a heart, our hearts.
Such thin ghosts. Keeping her soul company, botched &
belonging, from the necks of my brother, father, aunts,
uncles, niece, nephew, cousins, tenderness streaked—
little silver arrows. The dankest honey is grief.

[Dappled eggs in space. Chickens scratch constellations into blues]

*

Dappled eggs in space. Chickens scratch constellations into blues. In the clear glass ashtray, cherry pits. I was never one to trash existence or cry into my thoughts. Fact is, I soft-shoe shuffle through inner visions. Each silver that slivers. Each lunar landing, parts unknown. Even as Stephen Hawking predicts our shared Earth will breed parachutes of fire. Overhead, great whites will cinder bye-bye. We'll regrow extinct bird species in salt-pure labs. Just as whole heads of cabbage charbroil in the hills. Starbucks will charge a pinkie for a latte. & Just for funsies, we'll hologram celebrities onto our living room couch. Nicole Kidman will demand raw spinach smoothies & rap battles. No hand to hold (of course) in the afterlife & you'll have to loot a stranger's soul-points to stay alive.

[Hello Tuesday, soul-power pancakes]

*

Hello Tuesday, soul-power pancakes. After the mailwoman, my pooch is Fraggle Rock. Within the geode, an amphitheater of tin. Last December, powered down by bone cancer, my mother ceased. On Valentine's Day, Big Bryce flooded me with a text: "We have something new in common, K-Dawg." Mothers, dead. One month later, hours after smashing ping-pong, his nephew overdosed on pills. Then Liz lost each grandparent quickly, one by one, Daniel lost both parents in 2 weeks & Chris's younger brother died in his sleep Thanksgiving morning. Sometimes, life's nothing more than the brightness you shed. Inner mood commands, *Dissolve into sky*. How common. A lush drumming to nothing human without suspense.

[The things we carry—what to do?]

*

The things we carry—what to do? At the airport, on the way to my mother's hospice, I remember crying into a Big Mac. Hardly even shy about it. Denver Airport— Gate B29. *First no more grandparents, now "mother" is the absence I'll remodel for my life.* 2 children heaved chicken nuggets at the shoeshine. *They don't know they don't know.* Doc said, "Pelvis soft as cottage cheese. Get here soon. She won't last long." *Lord of darkness, give me the mask now.* Orange pill bottles, blueprint to her life. Expiration date mapped against a latticed future. Shaking like a quarry giving up. *Look mama, I'm a man without hands & my brain's a gin-smeared graveyard.* Terminal carpet, Coca-Cola stained. No passersby called my name in space or asked me where I hurt. Truth be told, so much of our suffering happens alone. Good fences making strangers of us all.

[Pigs in space, bacon-colored, sprouting wings]

*

Pigs in space, bacon-colored, sprouting wings &
departing home for hell. The root of travel is torture.
So what's the end to being, to being known? & Who are
we to be ourselves? (Consensus is Beyoncé's gonna live
forever & hush up all you haters.) Not so much a placing
as displacing—my neighbors body to body, half-hidden
in sheets—anything for them babies! He's wearing a
jaguar mask & mismatched socks & she strapped on
a fake gold halo. He trades futures part time on the
exchange & she micromanages a car wash for a living.
A bored labradoodle, saline tits & 1 slapping bed. Joy
makes the bird on fire. Shifting her throat muscles into
place, she's preparing to sing. A lovely tree sprouts in the
pollen-salted air of their intimacy. Into a white center, a
pressed square. Squeal like honey. His name, a season.
& Her pink world flowering reunions.

[Childhood's sweet, rotten gospel]

*

Childhood's sweet, rotten gospel, coloring my words &
tongue—Presbyterian, Methodist, Unitarian, Baptist,
on & on. May I learn to love again, for the first time.
White eternal of my comforter snowing my room—
bright flower, bright flower. Gutters, jamming with
fall's rot leaves. I pledge Allegiance. Mother's voice
keeps calling to me in dreams. Says, "In death we're
stronger than ourselves." (Our Maker, neither punitive
nor male.) Morning meditations into universal Love,
praying alone for everyone, yet I fail to feed the birds!
Eternities' shadows breed in my mind, raining a patch
on the shed's rusty nails. We're overlapping presences.
Jade rabbits enter purple heavens. There's *just* no cure
for that. I want to light every necktie on fire. I want to go
slopping 'round the ocean in a casket, amigo to whales,
reeking storms & ancient secrets.

[My whole house sweats blood]

*

My whole house sweats blood. Praying alone for everyone. World unglued, speak to me again. Speaking of horror, children permanently orphaned at the soul-divided border. *How have others become our pure hell?* Forming a human chain of complaints—broken social scene—our heart valves close. Love as my witness. To this America, how could I pledge Allegiance? *You have not manufactured my consent. You will not colonize my mind.* Father (to this day) promises he never wanted to be added to this country, forced to flee Vietnam as the war concluded with 2 purple hearts & blood-soaked socks. As a child, I cluelessly traced the spot a bullet entered his wrist with my pinky finger, relaxing in his lap. Bleach kit. Sorrow song. Broke blood cracking the whites of my eyes. I pledge Allegiance to family trees. Microbiomes. Kissing sprees. Hand-scrawled recipes stained with grease, passed up & down our generations.

[In the documentary on Aleppo]

*

In the documentary on Aleppo, concrete saws free
the miracle from the shadow of death. She's haloed in
dust. A salvaged, pint-sized, wailing infant. "All praise
to Allah." Our hearts applaud. I see 5 White Helmets
weeping into their armpits. 1 eye disbelieving what the
other eye distinctly sees. Imagine ultimate reality &
surrender. Imagine Abraham walking sacrificial Isaac
into the 2-hearted desert. The Virgin Mary appeared
to Bosnian children in a field of bright confusion. In
Lebanon, a girl cried crystals. The television medium
proclaims Aunt Susan's spirit is hovering behind us
& she wants us to know she hungers for strawberry
cheesecake. I wish I had that type of faith. To believe
we mend without a scar. Aubades burn below my skull's
domed roof.

[Grief flowers new dimensions]

*

Grief flowers new dimensions. Flooded rooms where our hearts live, hurting. Children, how alive you look in them leaves! *I wanna be lush in you that way.* Names of newborns identical to names craned into graves. I'm here for you, morning moon. Crescent honey-baby tending to the tide. Thanks for bringing me into being. For falling so cleanly through the gauze. In hot syrup, a red ant throbs. *What's my soul-age, now?* In the documentary, Shar (transgender / terminal diagnosis of Alzheimer's) starves herself to death, listens to "Strawberry Fields Forever" on repeat. Once a professor of numbers, she fails to count to 10. Slipped food by a nurse, she shakes her head *no!* Regions of deepest shatter are where we murmur. & When speech ends, the camera centers & holds steady on her gently thrashing chest.

[My neighbor reshingles his roof]

*

My neighbor reshingles his roof. A slipped hammer travels through his son to the ground. Decades without margins—oceans never stop. Funny how our hearts reflect their weathers. Nails jittering loose. The flesh of hours. It's hard to set down roots in rushing water. Violets ripen into storms. In *King Lear,* on the heath, nakedness howls. We learn the meanings of lose when we force ourselves to choose. Kangaroo court, he prosecutes barstools. Nightmare, beginning with a falsely manufactured threshold. Rattled down to zeros, Lear asks of Cordelia, "Why should a dog, a horse, a rat have life, / And thou no breath at all?" Poisoned pills, floating in his soul. He reminds me of a flashlight that no longer holds a charge. He reminds me there's just nothing to hold on to.

(How sad.)

Sometimes, we're just question marks to ourselves.

[What fool denies the inner life of a whale?]

*

What fool denies the inner life of a whale? Particles & waves, what's happening is a (her)story of fluid dynamics—beings plunging up & down through fractured light. Living ecology that cannot help but spread. Underground, flowers bloom, blue fire emergent. Child, lean a little toward the light. 14 hours each day, Chinese prison workers peel garlic. Fingernails sometimes worn down, sometimes missing. I'm a junkie of the *crazy wisdom tradition*. Applause for the riffraff, the fuckups, those who share my Tibetan master's tongue. I stroke the feathers that feed me. Would harness every living soul to mend you. Hello, washing machine, lush drumming to nothing, softening my sheets. Speaking of honest, my loose is tooth. Tell me the joke you speak with your whole being. The one ending in waterfalls spilling down a ladder.

[Masters from my spiritual tradition became so still]

*

Masters from my spiritual tradition became so still. They watched existence simmer in a tremendous, empty kettle. (Their hearts.) They watched it ALL from such great heights. Repeating, over & over, the Heart Sutra. To grow universal Love. Then headed home to simmer pots of jasmine rice. Hungry hospital voices call to me & (gently now) I touch each pain. *O mani padme hum.* Slip a dollar bill in the hungry palm of each beggar. Listen to bruises healing inside us. Plant a kiss on the forehead of the nearly departed. "On a scale of 1 to 10," mother said, "I'll be dead soon." (Brutal & unhinged.) All I could say was "I'm here for you. Just tell me where it hurts." Ask me to show up & I'll show up. Opening my arms into wild, uncut flowers. *May I be a vessel for her healing.* "The kingdom of God," Fred Rogers consoles, "is for the broken-hearted."

[In last night's dream, I collected my dead mother]

*

In last night's dream, I collected my dead mother in my arms. Sky overhead, where whole weather systems bruised & healed, bruised & healed. A single line you slurred, though your jawbone was deleted by the surgeons—"Being dead's like being alive, only a little different." The room was living & there you were, in it. (Fresh flying joy to hear your garbled voice. Of all things, a koan from your lips!) When I reached out to touch your back, you curlycued through the floorboards. Blue-gray smoke. Pepperidge Farm Goldfish floated through the room. (Ancestors returning from oblivion come back to *know* their voices.) Soft crown of bone, a crown of love. So much of being a being is want. *Have you found a god to worship in the afterlife? She wrathful or super chill? How many dreams of dears, beloveds until my mouth opens like sweet honey from a rock?*

[At the Oldorf Hospice House of Mercy]

*

At the Oldorf Hospice House of Mercy, our hearts outpaced our minds, blue-botched, unsewing. We shifted our knowing from room to room, heavy as Basho's winter apples or ice cliff moons. We wanted strength beyond black ice. In the bathroom, I failed to <slap> <slap> <slap> <slap> <slap> myself awake. Shiny chronograph of snow, running like a silver river down the streetlights. *Is it enough, to laugh through seasons, sizzle into atoms?* You asked to be cremated & we said (simply) yes. Then I carried your cremains in a box. How strange, the weight. What I hear is the last of you, mother, in the solemn boom of crows. How once you checked in faithfully each weekend & now I'm deleting your contact from my cell phone. Rocking back & forth in her sea, she last said, "Hi, Kevin." Not one word more. At suffering's end, she found a door.

[I now intensely cultivate universal love]

*

"I   now   intensely   cultivate
universal   love,   wishing
for   all   conscious   beings
only   true   happiness,   fulfillment,
peace   and   freedom   from   suffering.
I   experience   great   ecstatic   joy
at   the   very   thought   of   conscious   beings
abiding   forever   in   equanimity   and   bliss,
free   from   every   obvious   fear
and   subtle   anxiety.   As   universal   love
increases   in   the   mind   stream,
harmful   forces   cannot   affect   me,
and   I   become   a   protector
of   living   beings."

—Lex Hixon, *Mother of the Buddhas*

[My heart continues to digest mother's broken grammar]

*

My heart continues to digest mother's broken grammar. May I be a vessel for her healing. *Love, please complete each cell.* For all todays, let's let compassion lead. Deep attention is presence. A script with glittered gifts. Post-death McDonald's breakfast, biscuits & sloppy gravy, while mom rolled past on a stretcher, poorly hidden under a white sheet. We want our dears, beloveds alive in gentler heavens. Remembering my childhood home. She chain-smoked in deep gray shade. Opening the blinds, strictly prohibited. "They'll see me." Lightlessness to maim those poor houseplants. A humid I hated with nowhere to breathe. *How chronically alone she must have felt.* Still, wishing to bring her back, ancient crescent in my arms, singing Springsteen, always Springsteen, "Baby, we were born to run." How like redundancy's prisoner, pleading with life for more life, more life.

[Into each pore, we ask the world in]

Into each pore, we ask the world in. Traffic-controlling genetics machine who loves us most. Today, exiting my morning shower, I clearly saw (within my body) the body of all my relations. Ditch brims milkweed, wild sage, stinging nettle, mint, candy wrappers rinsed by cranky rains. It's the white, naked bowl that lets cherries—bloodred—bloom! At-home care, too tired for fear, mom rocked in a La-Z-Boy. Father & I cleaned her thighs with an orange sponge, vacuumed mucus from her lungs. A pure plane of silence we never dared to crease. I fed her mango smoothies, for the pain. Knowing she'd never pass this way again. What are we to our maker, that we must be shaped & mended, stricken & healed, over & over. Linus, speak to me of the blankets we carry.

["Every word," wrote Beckett, "is like an unnecessary stain"]

*

"Every word," wrote Beckett, "is like an unnecessary stain on silence and nothingness." He doubled down on this commitment, with conclusive force, when he died. Ripe with gallows humor, he was born on Good Friday. From Elie Wiesel comes the rebuttal—"We must always take sides. Neutrality helps the oppressor, never the victim. Silence encourages the tormentor, never the tormented." I know what I want, I want to chorus loud rains. To chant bye-bye to a crater of bruises. To love brutal beasts reeking of fresh kills. Sometimes, silence is the loudest weight. Like a body, wholly bodied at the brink. "I can't breathe!" Ain't it something now. My heart's the prayer the stars inherit. Jerked by every warning, every wonder. Cherry blossoms balancing the dark.

[Animals & stars were never ours to hold]

*

Animals & stars were never ours to hold dominion over. When asked how to teach children compassion, the Dalai Lama replied, "Teach them to like and respect insects." I wish a happy rebirth to each doomed pig. I pray *all* beings reach enlightenment & quickly. With all my heart & breath I wish them well, wanting each penned creature to find, at suffering's end, a door. Just as silence becomes part of the music. (Honest, though, I love breakfast bacon! & Pulled pork sandwiches. & Smokehouse brisket.) *Was I always this plump with unholy? A column of microbes & bone, longing for everyday miracles? Will I adjust my appetites so others can live?* All the things that died to keep me alive would pack Noah's ark floor to ceiling.

[*What would it mean, never to be brought into being?*]

*

What would it mean, never to be brought into being?
What would it mean to soul-sweat like this, forever?
Utnapishtim, bored as koalas, that's what. (Days when
all you can do is get blackout drunk, shift around
debris.) Some posit god a night-dark woman, Delta as
Louis Armstrong or Bessie Smith. The ocean dreams
in starfish. Blue whales. Hurricanes. Vampire squid.
Skyborne fish. Soon, all were singing. Cruel songs
fleshing the cold hearts' sorrow. & All the tender mercies
Love's unthawing. Holy honeysuckle! Let's make
mistakes. You can mistake god for a flashlight, church-
plump globes along your gospel path. Paramedics as
blue angels at the end of your 9-1-1. Horses melt in
kettles where no sleep blooms. Each frostburnt finger
longing toward a warmth.

[*Can we love life enough to anguish at its loss?*]

*

Can we love life enough to anguish at its loss? Precious human birth. Call it a *gift*. Even irony-free (if you can bear it.) I'm Weather Bear, trapped between mourning systems. It's hard to put down roots in running water. How the Stoics argue each of us (one soon day) will resolve into atomic blue dust. Each of us will be unavailable currency in our grandchildren's toothless mouths. Afternoons we spent slashing the throats of unsuspecting flowers. *Aurelius, how can we love this life with our whole heart?* (Lost blueprint of being.) (Future shock & the map frosted over.) (Erasure City.) "The good news," said Master, "is that there's nothing to hold on to." Colorful nonsense. Einstein's brain suspended in a jar at the Mütter Museum. I can't F-U-C-K-I-N-G breathe. (C'mon, universe, shuttle me some air!) Trying to stuff my body back in my body, I would slash seams.

[Our sky of sudden hail]

*

Our sky of sudden hail. Our soul dyslexia. Our cruel teasing nicknames. Our crime sprees, just to keep breathing. Our American failure to matter to each other (even to ourselves). Our *I'm sorry for your loss.* Our complicated edge. Our luminous death trips over deep-fried Snickers. Our snug-as-a-bug in a world so bad. Our chain-smoking nurses, shivering in goose feathers as it snows. Our algebraic coefficient. Our "best cultural practices." Our mouths full of "fuck yes." Our racist president & big sad juice. Our self-deportation & gene edits. Our stolen guns popping off toward heaven. Our Beyoncé & broke-off teeth. Our unused tears in the brutal migration. Our salvation figures, hung in cages above the drama. Our next Buddha will be a sangha.

[Our White Helmets tranced by the blast]

*

Our White Helmets tranced by the blast. Our microbiomes full of cadences. Our self-bleaching at the level of the soul, just to smooth in. Our ship of unkissed hippos. Our gene pools uploaded to cyber. Our anger burning all tenderness away. Our rookie forensic investigators. Our slaughterhouse futures. Our procession of supermarket oranges to the ground. Our *Dear Apocalypse,* . . . Our honey burning wild in a circle. Our doing it all with rancid runny hearts. Our body-cam footage. Our hot-pink mottled thunder. Our rubber bumpers down the heart's loose walls. (*It's been a long life. It's been a long life.*) Our synchronized breathing. Our chalk outlines ascending from freshly poured pavement. Our moon commanding each wave (& they obey).

[Our Declaration of Interdependence]

*

Our Declaration of Interdependence. Our Black Lives Matter. Our kiddos, knighting each owl, one by one. Our bodies' littered interiors. Our soap opera addiction & shitting, clapping babies. Our salvation figures big as brontosauruses. Our thick Book of Feuds. Our Walmart Supercenter, in ruins. Our kingdom of great Zen circles. Our white chalk outlines, warmth in recession. Our "leaked" celebrity sex tapes. Our cherry rockets, racing past moons. Our penned, doomed pigs & wonderlust. Our vast empty hearts & cherry blossoms. Our kiss on the forehead of 1 who has left us. Our whale of a car crash. Our continuous prayer for now.

[In the multiverse, other versions of ourselves]

*

In the multiverse, other versions of ourselves. Another Kevin who underapplies sunscreen, plants pinks, darkens to Delta, researches Rimsky-Korsakov, binges Singapore-street-food videos on YouTube, photographs goats, praises the riffraff & lists away despite each emerald warning. Despite each medication for each pain. Bloodred moon wired to the tide. Another me with birthmarks longing to be kissed. It's all around me now. Feelings of sweet action ice cream. Ephemeral, crazy rants of weightless sweetness. The river of my dreams flying to pieces. In the next heaven, icy neon lightning. In the next heaven, no more guns. No more body bags rising from the asphalt chops. Only dirty little angel choirs burning in a circle, lost in a round.

[& When I arrived at my mother's deathbed]

*

& When I arrived at my mother's deathbed, I pledged Allegiance. Her (barely there, barely there) sad-hurt filled my whelmed heart 'til my one true want was a longing to come to the end of shaming. O permanent impermanence, to be magical no more. The moon was a flashlight held by a cosmic nurse. Said, "Just tell me where it hurts." Everywhere. Me Pozzo & you Lucky, waiting for Godot. Another no-show. FUCK cancer. FUCK death & bodies harvested piecemeal, language scrambled to coos. Potassium deficiencies. Radiation, wholly unnecessary surgeries. Pills & pills, pills all the way down. 3 new medications for each pain. Mother, you sang so quietly into your death. How your body died from your toes to neck, yet your brain (somehow) lived on. Your exhales creased the air another 7 hours. *What a lesson.* No salvation figures big as bouncers would bring you back.

[Seas & stars were never ours to hold dominion over]

*

Seas & stars were never ours to hold dominion over.
Try (if you can manage) a *yes* with your whole heart.
Your whole heart, it's nothing real. Your whole heart, a
cow-plump pasture. Your whole heart, part Thelonious
Monk, part Thich Nhat Hanh. Evenings we washed
thunder from open cuts. Tremulous like a quarry giving
up. They put a bandana over the elephant's eyes & it
stopped her shaking. Gently handled, restored to soft.
Each time we say, *Goodnight, neighbor, sweet dreams
in gentler heavens,* we're deathless for now. Scarlessly
closing like water over water. Save them tears, little
cow, little cow. Against the sunrise, a blood orange in
my cupped palms.

[Myths, a script of gifts for the living]

*

Myths, a script of gifts for the living. Said Chögyam Trungpa, "We have wonderful backgrounds." In the cosmic ocean incubator, jellyfish dream our living into being. We dream them back in high resolution—a mirrored circle—yet I fail to feed the birds! Listen on. Monday, 23rd of November, 1654. Blaise Pascal. Smoldering in all his cells. Blowing open to nowhere living. Licked metaphysical honey from the palms of Abraham, Isaac, Jacob & Jesus. Blast furnace heart. He braided his soul-force to the soul-force of G-d. The sweetest weld. The sweetest weld. I'd like to think G-d dreamed him back. Lined him with Psalms & taught him to cry. Broke his kneecaps to show him Andromeda. For me, amoebas are enough wonder to smash my brain. Nina Simone falls through me like mending rain. Our hearts, the truest north worth closely knowing.

[In every life, a moment or 2, for heaven's sake]

*

In every life, a moment or 2, for heaven's sake. "Pregnant jade rabbit enters purple heaven." Oooooooohhhhhhhhh! Why've I never encountered such mysteries before? Teeth marks we leave in the world's strange heart. Unasked, unthanked. Upstairs, asleep, my roommates—heart-to-heart—dream into the collective. Orson teaches 300 walruses synchronized swimming under a skyline dancing icy neon moons. Brooke dreams of grapefruit burning angry at the bottom of a well. Miranda wades waist-deep in hot-pink, sticky goldfish. Present moments furred with last night's dreams. "I cannot understand why my arm is not a lilac tree," says Leonard Cohen. *At what point does living become surreal?*

[Among artists frozen into snowbanks]

*

Among artists frozen into snowbanks, among riot shields & drone strikes, no. 3 main ballast tanks, *hands up, don't shoot,* blue moon hydrangea, tearjerkers & riffraff, a whale of a car crash, Aleppo in ruins, another new crime spree, sidewalk vomit, pizza-chef migraines, the feathers that feed us, kindness forgiving 1 day for the next, let's dance in the river before we go home, then wait. Wait—for ghosts to be rinsed clean in the light, for the Discovery Channel to reveal, for savior figures big as bouncers, for forensics to be shipped back from the lab, for shotgun fire to dissolve into flowers mid-flight. Another colored body growing colder. One headline [adds to / complicates / hides / reveals / replaces] another, grief translated into anger, something always on fire, vacant fire extinguisher, beneath bridges, in libraries, under stairwells, frostburnt transients slip in needles. Say yes.

[Yes. Hours brighten into months]

*

Yes. Hours brighten into months, knives saw clean
through flesh, let fish swim through hoops of light,
cocaine energize our spectrums, bright rabbit blood
race to the moon, let the aspens shiver their fuckyes, let
the river answer, first & foremost, let her answer. An ear
of listening to the earth—can you hear them? Listen on.
Can you hear them? They're saying, *They snapshot my
terror before emptying their guns,* saying, *I reached out
completely to every hurting heart & my heart also hurt,*
saying, *We cut ourselves on sharp & rough, they say
sweet sticky asphalt, I'm down on my knees waiting
for the Lord to come—please come,* saying, *Traded in 2
dollars for a nasty can of Coke.*

[*Can you hear them?*]

*

Can you hear them? Deaf ear, put your listening to the ground. The sound you hear is questions bleeding through the wall. One by one we chant to see it broken. Steel-wide & thick, white failing. Rib cage where our hearts went missing. This story is pollution. Imagine home, a somewhere for every someone, praise for the riffraff, February forgiveness parades, transitions between genders, enough soul-fire to clear off a layer of dead skin. It's how we *really* make America great again. Even the man walking down the street blasted on discount vodka longs to be home. Listen, he's singing (this time) of apples & blankets, moonshine & hickeys—(this deadbeat eyesore)—& soon he, too, will drop to one knee & collapse in human laughter.

[We travel to our shipping address, like all things]

*

We travel to our shipping address, like all things, for as long as the glue holds. Fish & chips with dollar draws. We anatomize adhesion. No *return to sender*. Impossible to say where the premonition of death comes from. 1 strain of jellyfish can live forever, slowly self-regenerating cell by cell. Once an elder, she's embryonic once more. If 1 factor must sway the decision, let it be joy! Joy sails the bird to fire. Loads of glitter jammed into the gills of hills. *What is the end to being, to being known?* A hospital declares itself dead with orders to "do not resuscitate." 1 fugue of Shostakovich, 2 chewing flies, 1 ship of botched birds, another whale of a truck wreck. Say what you will—say virtually anything—just please don't command me to *wait*. (Dozing in traffic, huffing smog, idling away.) No need (now) to set down roots in running water.

[We who boil in space]

*

We who boil in space. We who pledge Allegiance. "Build the wall." A trove of feathers clash & bleed in the anxious sun. *Mother Buddha, do we hunger where we matter? Are you busy dragging caravans beyond gravity, into heaven? Everything okay?* In this knotting down to tribes I would scrub-scrub-scrub away seams. I see you. Swelled human cargo. 18-wheel erasures. Wounds shuffling at the militarized border. White blessed rage burning *all* tenderness away. Oh look, a set of socks the shape of my own lost feet. "If we meet each other in Hell," argues Geoffrey Hill, "it's not Hell." *Can you hear them? Can I trust you'll care?* This is just to say. Compassion becomes the brightest weight. I'm going to join each of you in Hell & howl your names into this deafness.

[So we traveled hand in hand through time]

*

So we traveled hand in hand through time, 'til cancer wintered in. *Mother, why were you never inclined to make friends / want friends?* A pharmacy to adjust every fire. Sick as you lived much of your adult life—I never blushed as you self-medicated with booze, as you failed to matter (even to yourself). Bedroom locked & chugging vodka, howling, "Fuck the fuck off!" & Those voicemails. Voicemails. Cartography of despair. At 4 a.m. At 4:05 a.m. 4:17. 5:39. Sometimes, a dozen in a weekend. Said, "Your brother's a real puke. You know that? He thinks he's king. He's king of nothing living. Please. Show some respect! & Call your mother, Kevin, when you get this. [Takes a long drag from a cigarette, exhales.] So many fingers god gave ya & ya ain't even using them." (*Momma, I knew everywhere you hurt.*)

[We who open into prayer]

We who open into prayer. We who collage sage. Conduct strawberry jam ceremonials. The volume of our hearts careening inside a slaughterhouse. (Hook rows, symmetrical as church pews.) Ham hocks floating from killing floors to supermarket shelves. *So much of living is living off loss.* We who are tethered to mothers' brutal strokes. Dumpsters rimmed with elegiac bees. What a knowing. *Hush, you lush, torqued crying. Time's just no forever. Sad, doomed child. Wake the hell up!* Some soon tomorrow I, too, will perish. In wordless terror. Grandpa did. Hours after wrangling cold, lost moons into his hospital room & maligned their hearts with savage little questions. What a lesson. Each faithful name that time in time simply unlearns.

[Just as time erases kisses from my body]

*

Just as time erases kisses from my body. Just as my family bows down to sadness & cancer. & I fall through dreams rehearsing the Dictionary of Distant Angels. & Rise from morning hay, clean as a salt lick, in a field of long division. I pray alone for everyone, recalling *The Diamond Sutra*. "However many beings there are in whatever realms of being might exist, whether they are born from an egg or born from a womb, born from the water or born from the air, whether they have form or no form, whether they have perception or no perception or neither perception nor no perception, in whatever conceivable realm of being one might conceive of beings, in the realm of complete nirvana, I shall liberate them all. And though I thus liberate countless beings, not a single being is liberated."

[Everything's just 1 insight]

*

Everything's just 1 insight. What a lesson. Mother's body simplified to atoms, scooped into a box. Bleach kit. Want song. A whole world we lost in the fire. Night bears unscrewed their heads. Honey-kissed prayers dispatched to kingdom come. Whiskey empties overflowed my bedroom trash can. Common pipeline to shipwreck. Drunk pink soul-salts in a lake of long division. I know you. Grief-without-ceasing. Blossoms giggled into / out of time. (We edged mother's cremains with pine needles, returned ashes to earth.) Velvet sky mounting as it crashed in our laps. Leaving our hungry palms wet. *Jade rabbit enters purple heaven.* She don't-know-she-don't-know. This is just to say. She don't-know-she-don't-know. *What can't God-my-Mother know?* Anything. What a lesson. Furred silence leaked from a creek of long division. *Since when did loving become* this *unnatural?*

[What if love is just spondees]

*

What if love is just spondees. What if winds bleed anxious down a string. What if the sun demands a fresh coat of paint. What if I'm just chicken cluck & stormed complaints. What if the unicorn is black. What if enlightenment's pure-grade horseshit. What if we know mangoes for the first time. What if silence is the loudest prize. What if we upload our souls & the servers crash. What if god's popping prescription meds. What if pig's foot. What if soul-division. What if we heal slow motion, when we heal at all. & The reason is sweet maple, like the flow down our necks. & We hear silence as part of the music. What if there's no more moo shu pork. What if, in heaven, there are no doors.

[We compassion]

*

We compassion. To muddy ledges. Storm pinks. Blossom space. *Danse nue.* Misquote Nietzsche. Pull moonshine acres to ground control. *Is this thing live?* How we tattoo ancestors with shipping labels. Donate souls to live on elsewhere. No *return to sender.* Just us buckling. Within prayers. Though no one's around. & To be alive is to spill out of these cuts. Our master's myths maturing into dust. *Remember how we failed love? Chained-up space? Stained neckties & cheap lingerie? Overflowed trashcans with cheap champagne? Poisoned Now & Laters?* Look, they're mine now. Mine. Every dearly beloved. Vast lonesome terrors. Each spoon-fed medication for each pain. *Are there no exit doors but these?* Huddled fingers longing toward a warmth. Each heat recedes. A drift of hours bluing frostburnt fingers.

[We command assertions of value]

*

We command assertions of value. We sour where we
hunger. & Blister along a plane of many dots. Despite
our efforts to connect, we still feel haunted by lonely.
Zeros with decommissioned superheroes. Lost in space,
bowling alone. We add in Oprah. (Tepid applause.)
Beyoncé! (God yes, hallelujah!) & Geolocating bats.
(Percussive distance.) Now add all the public parks to
kiss in. Sea-salted intimacy twisting through a season.
(Babies!) "Pull a thread here," said Nadeem Aslam, "and
you'll find it's attached to the rest of the world." Now
add a crater with shattered branches, legless horses,
an eyeless tiger with nothing living on 1 half, frogs
with 3 heads but no legs. Add a farmhouse where all
the circling wolves burn red. 6-ring beer connectors.
Selenium. Lithium ion. Beings on earth tangled in our
weather. With nothing to hold on to. *Is this thing live?*

[Confession]

*

Confession. We don't know how to add inmates with extinguished souls so we add criminals with x'ed out eyes. (You get the picture.) Then backfill the scene with stinking mustard jungles. Nurses pocketing patient pills. (Some shared diagnosis.) Add in moo shu pork, 2 sides of fried rice. Quarter draws. Mangoes becoming mangoes for the first time. (Ripeness is all!) We kiss the earth in child's pose. Daydrunk before noon. Whiskey & kisses everywhere. Hickeys bleeding up our necks. Supermoons we balanced on a stick. (What a lesson.) Add in surgery & dearly beloveds. Valves stuck open. An animal's chronic prayers to nothing living. Failed blood transfusions. Charlie Chaplin & laughing bananas. IV tubes cocooning the body in soft. (A nest.) In this version of eternity, they're offering soul-upgrades. We keep our rage domestic. (What a cost!)

[*Mother, I've built a hospital*]

*

Mother, I've built a hospital for this family of hail-smashed birds. [   ] *& Shined down more orphaned blackbirds for these nurses to heal.* [   ] *If only this ruckus of cancers would lie down in a calm. (Please calm.)* [   ] *'Round my grief I drew circles with a stick in the dirt. Wanted something impossible. A living I held vast dominion over.* [   ] *(In pleated waves—above & through the cells of my being—it soon spread.)* [   ] *In last night's dream, the submarine captain yelled, "STICK-'EM-UP!" Red robbery melted down walls. I hid my heart in my heart. Concealed both hearts in my mouth. Stapled shut my lips. Dead, eyeless birds floated past the grease-smeared portholes.* [   ] *Mother, are extinct birds in heaven now, growing eternal feathers? Fresh skin?* [   ] *Tell me, are we mended as we enter? Everything okay?*

[Raw honey sun]

*

Raw honey sun. Champagne mangoes. Jeweled pig eyes. (Say it, Kev!) Everyday miracles = a purple, rippled thunder! Leaving our present paradise for address unknown. Living far west of myself, once-upon-a-grief, I was thoroughly snowed in. Cocooned in a network of scarves & ceaseless polyrhythms. Treasuring self-silence, I nursed anguish, hid. Today, inner moons wake up from within. 1 by 1. & All around me now. Each a softer wonder than the last. "The good news," says Master, "is that there's nothing to hold on to." This is just to say / I'm starving / each seed of self-shame, / the calloused gravity / of *no*s. You shouldn't have to cry every day just because you exist. I pledge Allegiance. To each erased species. Compassion's arrow. Bottomless forgiveness. Each name that time (in time) simply unlearns.

[Said simply]

*

Said simply. Sinuous nudes recline into each other.
Said simply. The sum on all wavelengths. Down our
faces, sunglasses collapse. We crease. To the ruptures
of babies. Compassion's our *Reading Rainbow*—a
leaky yellow highlighter down our hours. Making living
legible. Connection sustainable. Speaking of honest, my
loose is tooth. Dears, beloveds. When (last) did you chase
rubber duckies in the ocean? Braid the words of your
favorite book to your heart? Unlatch your jaw to seed
the dying earth with your song? (The singer becoming
the chorus becoming the vision.) I know what I want. I
want to root in the shadows the moon keeps dropping.
To fill my begging bowl with cherry blossoms. To invite
snapdragons to blossom everywhere all at once. (Pillow
thoughts.) Mother says, *Sweet child, what on earth you
been thinking?* Says, *Child, please stop gluing fractures
to the fractures. I wanted it broken.* Says, *All of this
existence I've gifted you & you chose to freeze between
frames without hands on the lawn?*

[Imagine meditations on meditation]

*

Imagine meditations on meditation   *   Sun salutations
& freaky soul-hydration   *   A room of neon walruses
migrating into smoke   *   Imagine waking & waking
up (strange, high listenings, souls to ground)   *   Vast
blue knowing, honey breathing in the rocks   *   1 crystal
pony / 1 life jacket washed in the flood / 1 bird ghost
raced into cyber   *   Firing prayer after prayer into
heaven's purple, glistening guts   *   Skyscrapers cry
glass as they melt to the ground   *   *Can you hear me
now? Is this thing live?*   *   Late breaking versions of
rapture, ours for a cost   *   *If rest can be had on this
earth, may I lay down in a calm*   *   Sweet Buddhas
*   Sweet moldy raspberries   *   Flaws braiding our
code   *   Dank purple thunders drumming up & down
our lawn

[Sprouted splinter fevers]

*

Sprouted splinter fevers   *   Migrated between after-parties & bars of bitter chocolate   *   The radio scientist warns, "1.3 billion years of genetic evolutionary history has already been erased"   *   So many zeros stampeding through the room   *   It's the shape my mouth makes, hurting   *   Better than that other thing (to be nowhere & nothing at all)   *   Dreamed of being post-human—a lilac tree littered with critters, a supervolcano with extravagant birthdays, preparing to launch   *   The sun's an orange the sky keeps smoking   *   I drew in a tangled breath & shipped yet another species off to heaven with regret   *   Knowing what must be known, what I cannot fully know despite all of this life: other earthlings have it worse (mine's been a charmed life)

[Everything priests promised was eternal]

*

Everything priests promised was eternal—hot-pink cotton candy bleeding through our palms   *   Make no mistake—all I'm asking for is to be stuffed with 1 more helping of champagne mango & beef shank & perfectly phrased 18th-century haiku before my heart beats loud & Shiva stacks a dozen pine cones in my skull   * Magnetic sky clouding with bruises—it's my mind   * Each bruise a sick little flower blown apart in crossing wind   *   Magic markers breathe inside us or (wait) is that *just* another wind?   *   If eternity can be mothered, call it ours   *   In dreams, we sport puffy flying jetpacks, playing cosmic tag among diamonds that flame against the rim   *   Floating points in a freeze of cloudy dots   * "You're it, no you're it. You're it, no you're it!"   *   With all the diamonds singing   *   Diamonds on diamonds, all the way down   *   Once again with nothing to hold on to

[I didn't even get the chance to kiss you goodbye]

*

I didn't even get the chance to kiss you goodbye,
Passenger Pigeon, Ryukyu Woodpigeon, Réunion Pink
Pigeon. I didn't even get the chance to kiss you goodbye,
Elephant Bird, Upland Moa, King Island Emu. I didn't
even get the chance to kiss you goodbye, Amsterdam
Island Duck, Pink-Headed Duck, Great Spotted Kiwi.
I didn't even get the chance to kiss you goodbye,
Auckland Islands Merganser, New Zealand Quail,
Himalayan Quail. I didn't even get the chance to kiss you
goodbye, Javanese Lapwing, White-Winged Sandpiper,
North Island Snipe. I didn't even get the chance to
kiss you goodbye, South Island Snipe, Canadian Black
Oystercatcher, Bar-Winged Rail. I didn't even get the
chance to kiss you goodbye, Tahiti Rail, North Island
Bush Wren, Réunion Rail. I didn't even get the chance
to kiss you goodbye, Miller's Rail, Samoan Wood Rail,
Bermuda Night Heron. I didn't even get the chance to
kiss you goodbye, Ascension Night Heron, Bermuda
Shearwater, Guadalupe Storm-Petrel.

[I didn't even get the chance to kiss you goodbye]

*

I didn't even get the chance to kiss you goodbye, Sulu Bleeding-Heart, Red-Mustached Fruit-Dove, Negros Fruit-Dove. I didn't even get the chance to kiss you goodbye, Paradise Parrot, Cuban Red Macaw, Carolina Parakeet. I didn't even get the chance to kiss you goodbye, Coppery Thorntail, Turquoise-Throated Puffleg, Imperial Woodpecker. I didn't even get the chance to kiss you goodbye, Ivory-Billed Woodpecker, Mangarevan Whistler, Western Victorian Pied Currawong. I didn't even get the chance to kiss you goodbye, White-Eyed River Martin, Red Sea Swallow, Bay Starling. I didn't even get the chance to kiss you goodbye, Bourbon-Crested Starling, Cozumel Thrasher, Slender-Billed Grackle. I didn't even get the chance to kiss you goodbye, Réunion Fody, Tawny-Headed Mountain-Finch, Hooded Seedeater. I didn't even get the chance to kiss you goodbye, Réunion Kestrel, Réunion Owl, Laughing Owl.

[*Do you believe in magic?*]

*

*Do you believe in magic? 21st-century miracles?
Dime-sized miracles to whelm human souls?* Eternity
sprouting wings on our behalf. "All that I am, or hope to
be," said Abraham Lincoln, "I owe to my angel mother."
So add in angels. American angels. Angels above East
St. Louis. Shreveport. Denver. Angels demolishing
mac 'n' cheese on our behalf. Jack & Coke–mixing
angels. Angels rehearsing tongue twisters & dying for
1 last smoke. Angels sorting souls in unmarked graves.
Shipping forensics back to the lab. *Dears, beloveds, can
you hear them?* They're jailbreaking science, hunting
for a cure. They're misquoting Wittgenstein in the off-
hours. Selling slaughterhouse futures—everything's
Zen. Their meditations are crippled rivers & all the leaves
rise, wet. They demand their coffee black. Construction
worker angels, reeking tar. Hospice angels, putting
whole worlds to bed. *Can you hear them?* Listen on.
They're asking where it hurts even as they also hurt. Call
them Quan Yin, Avalokiteshvara, Mother Mary—their
changing, sudden names. Loving chants ripple down
the hours.

["Suffering is part of the divine idea."]

*

"Suffering is part of the divine idea" (Henry Ward Beecher). "Affliction is a treasure, and scarce any man hath enough of it" (John Donne). "Out of suffering have emerged the strongest souls; the most massive characters are seared with scars" (Khalil Gibran). Men's appetite for self-martyrdom failed to amuse my mother. Born into a marked body, she never exclaimed, *Go on & praise the hell that is this body. Thank you, lords, for this, my shipwreck!* Nor did she believe our world divinely ordered. Local joys, like wanting to be wanted, was (for her) enough. Or so I mused, dressing her wounds with Neosporin, blending mango smoothies she learned to love, wheeling her down the hospital hallway post-radiation, gently over bumps. *Let me be a vessel for her healing. Yet let the end come quickly, when it must.* "I can sympathize with everything," reasoned Oscar Wilde, "except suffering."

[Said simply]

Said simply. I would ship myself naked in a splintery wood crate halfway across the universe, harnessed to the back of an asthmatic, wheezing space camel, just to say face-to-face, "Mother, I've missed you in regions of my heart I didn't know existed while you lived. Each day your loss rivers through me. All the things are colored by your loss. Your strange magic was yours alone & when you died it became a teal river in my sky. It's all around me now. A sad, living weather I can't unknow. Perhaps, in time, I won't wish to match myself to nothingness, to compassion past the brink. I would trade 3 years of crying for 3 fresh hours, for 2 fresh-squeezed hours, for *just* 1 hour with you by my side & all the beasts sprinting through the hills."

[*I drank the whole alphabet of grief. Then held a blood orange*]

*

I drank the whole alphabet of grief. Then held a blood orange in my cupped palm against the sun & begged for a new young moon. For the moon, she commands each wave (& they obey). [   ]   *Every anxious wave.* [   ]   *Mother, were you the first god given to me as a child?* [   ]   *Is it foolish to consider eternity payment for this life? (If I had existed before, wouldn't I know without having to be told?)* [   ]   *The flesh of hours racing through the seasons.* [   ]   *"Mother, if you're somewhere, please know the lengths we've grown from you," tenderness making transients of us all.* [   ]   *Now every shrine I build for you teaches me to kneel.* [   ]   *Look at me, I'm all knees.* [   ]   *Everything I never said I can't smooth in.* [   ]   *In death, are you completed by silence?* [   ]   *Or are you flying through afterlives in a cherry-red race car, fueled by cappuccino & your imagination?* [   ]   *Come on, all you ghosts. Every ancestor in every heaven.* [   ]   *In whatever form, whatever dimension, won't you come out?*

[Brothers, sisters, impossible to say]

*

Brothers, sisters, impossible to say (if I / if we) will be graced with an afterlife. But if living is more than the sum of these cells, for my next life I'd like to be a cherry blossom, giggled into space next to a stone Buddha. Next, perhaps, a hospital nurse, cocooning "at risk" worlds in soft. & For my next act, let me become braids of wind over a Milk Moon river. Or a stoic goddess, in a bat-filled cave, restored to grace below these human dramas. Let me become a cosmic rabbit sprinting in & out of heaven. A sky of dirty valentines dropping cold confetti kisses. Let me become healing forces in a field of long division. Or a cosmic pig with extended wings flying through the burning.

[Dears. Beloveds]

*

Dears. Beloveds. Return the shovel to the shed—the grave is over. Down this clear glad river we float. Feeling good lost. Somewhere, in silk-light water, lucent deathless jellyfish. Just not us. In the ultrasound photo, a bunched-up fist. Tonight, let's circle the floodwaters, find perfect stones to skip across the light. Let us imagine. Love is the light now. Or we could voyage down this lush blue flood strapped into life jackets—stars overhead shooting cells of light at one another (cosmic tag)—& watch this little opera, faults & all.

Falling   gently   ever   gently

to the sounds.

[Closing waves]

*

Closing   waves:

"The   supremely   subtle
fundamental   innate
Mind   of   Clear   Light
is   all   goodness.
It   has   no   beginning   or   end.
It   constantly   emanates   the   dance
of   compassion   and   wisdom,
performed   by   oceans   of   Awakened   Ones
and   their   daughters   and   sons
who pervade innumerable   dimensions. . . .

Abiding   in   the   primordial   peace
of   the   natural   purity   of   all   phenomena,
a   fortunate   one   am   I
who   seeks   Great   Bliss.
May   I   be   a   vessel   for   the   nectar
of   Secret   Mantra—to   help   all   beings,
in   all   worlds,   in   all   ways."

—Lex Hixon, *Mother of the Buddhas*

70

Notes

[I pass through the mental hospital]: *"May I help all beings, in all worlds, in all ways"* is from Lex Hixon's *Mother of the Buddhas: Meditation on the Prajnaparamita Sutra.*

[Sweet jumping Jesus, bright flocks of rain!]: "& Even with Buddha as pilot, flying still gives me the shakes" is inspired by a sentence in Melissa Kwasny's *The Nine Senses:* "If Walt Whitman were the pilot, I wouldn't be afraid to fly."

[Eternal waves quarrel at the bottom of a well full of blueness]: "Build the wall" is attributed to Donald Trump.

[Beneath dark purples, new life jockeying through the cracks]: "It's a beautiful day in the neighborhood . . . Won't you be my neighbor?" comes from Fred Rogers's song "Won't You Be My Neighbor." "Build the wall" is, again, attributed to Donald Trump.

[What brought us from the ocean into diamond Buddhafields?]: "The artist is extremely lucky who is presented with the worst possible ordeal which will not actually kill him" is attributed to John Berryman from a 1972 interview in the *Paris Review.*

[In the documentary on Aleppo]: Parts of this poem are inspired by the documentary *The White Helmets* (2016).

[Grief flowers new dimensions]: Parts of this poem are inspired by the documentary *Tomorrow Never Knows,* by Adam Sekuler, in the film MFA program at the University of Colorado, Boulder.

[My neighbor reshingles his roof]: "Why should a dog, a horse, a rat have life, / And thou no breath at all?" is from Shakespeare's *King Lear.*

[At the Oldorf Hospice House of Mercy]: "At suffering's end, she found a door" is inspired by a line in Louise Glück's poem "The Wild Iris": "At the end of my suffering / there was a door."

[I now intensely cultivate universal love]: This poem takes its text from Lex Hixon's *Mother of the Buddhas: Meditation on the Prajna-paramita Sutra.*

[My heart continues to digest mother's broken grammar]: "Baby, we were born to run" comes from Bruce Springsteen's song "Born to Run."

["Every word," wrote Beckett, "is like an unnecessary stain"]: The titular quote is attributed Samuel Beckett. "We must always take sides. Neutrality helps the oppressor, never the victim. Silence encourages the tormentor, never the tormented" is from Elie Wiesel's *From the Kingdom of Memory: Reminiscences.*

[Animals & stars were never ours to hold]: "Teach them to like and respect insects" is attributed to the Dalai Lama. "[A]t suffering's end, a door" is, again, inspired by a line in Louise Glück's poem "The Wild Iris": "At the end of my suffering / there was a door."

[*Can we love life enough to anguish at its loss?*]: This poem was inspired by a Chögyam Trungpa quote: "The bad news is you're falling through the air, nothing to hang on to, no parachute. The good news is, there's no ground."

[**Myths, a script of gifts for the living**]: "We have wonderful backgrounds" is from Chögyam Trungpa's *The Sanity We Are Born With: A Buddhist Approach to Psychology.*

[**In every life, a moment or 2, for heaven's sake**]: "I cannot understand why my arm is not a lilac tree" is a quote from Leonard Cohen's *Beautiful Losers.*

[**We who boil in space**]: "If we meet each other in Hell / it's not Hell" is from Geoffrey Hill's *Broken Hierarchies: Poems 1952–2012.* "Build the wall" is attributed to Donald Trump.

[**Just as time erases kisses from my body**]: "However many beings there are in whatever realms of being might exist, whether they are born from an egg or born from a womb, born from the water or born from the air, whether they have form or no form, whether they have perception or no perception or neither perception nor no perception, in whatever conceivable realm of being one might conceive of beings, in the realm of complete nirvana, I shall liberate them all. And though I thus liberate countless beings, not a single being is liberated" is from Red Pine's *The Diamond Sutra.*

[We command assertions of value]: "Pull a thread here and you'll find it's attached to the rest of the world" is from Nadeem Aslam's *The Wasted Vigil*.

[Closing waves]: This prayer takes its text from Lex Hixon's *Mother of the Buddhas: Meditation on the Prajnaparamita Sutra*.

Acknowledgments

Thanks to the incredible journals where the following poems were first given life, sometimes in a different form or with an alternate title:

Gulf Coast: "[Outside the snapdragons, cords of light]," "[To witness a selkie, owl-grandmother, grief]" & "[Dears. Beloveds]"

Cave Wall: "[I pass through the mental hospital]" & "[Into each pore, we ask the world in]"

Barrow Street: "[Sweet jumping Jesus, bright flocks of rain!]"

Colorado Review: "[Beneath dark purples, new life jockeying through the cracks]," "[My neighbor re-shingles his roof]" & "[What if love is just spondees]"

PANK: "[Kombucha & skincare]," "[Childhood's sweet, rotten gospel]" & "[Just as times erases kisses from my body]"

Prairie Schooner: "[I walk past the mental hospital]" & "[The things we carry—what to do?]"

Salt Hill: "[Grief flowers new dimensions]"

The *Georgia Review:* "[What fool denies the inner life of a whale?]"

Potomac Review: "[Masters from my spiritual tradition became so still]"

Bellingham Review: "[In last night's dream, I collected my dead mother]," "['Every word,' Beckett wrote, 'is like an unnecessary stain']" & "[In every life, a moment or two, for heaven's sake]"

Notre Dame Review: "[At Oldorf's Hospice House of Mercy]"

The *Florida Review:* "[Our sky of sudden hail]"

The *Cincinnati Review:* "[Among artists frozen into snowbanks],""[Yes. Hours, brighten into months]" & "[Can you hear them?]"

North American Review: "[We travel to our shipping address, like all things]"

Quarterly West: "[Everything's just one insight]"

Poetry Northwest: "[Do you believe in magic?]"

Thanks, also, to Cate Marvin for including the pieces "[Among artists frozen into snowbanks]," "[Yes. Hours, brighten into months]" & "[Can you hear them?]" in the 2020 edition of *Best New Poets.*

Infinite gratitude to *Black Warrior Review* for including 37 pages from this manuscript—my chapbook *Closing Waves*—in their Fall/Winter 2019 (46.1) edition.

To each, to all, I feel great & ecstatic joy for inclusion in your pages.

I would like to express my deep thanks, as well, to the many people & institutions that have so generously supported my writing: The Helen Zell Writers' Program at the University of Michigan, the University of Iowa, Martha's Vineyard Institute for Creative Writing, Bucknell Seminar for Younger Poets, the National Endowment for the Arts, and my editors Stephanie G'Schwind, Jess Turner & Donald Revell.

I offer my ongoing thanks to those who have so thoughtfully read and responded to my poetry along the way: Ruth Awad, Keith Taylor, Laura Kasischke, Linda Gregerson, Lorna Goodison, Ben Doller, Michael Dumanis, Joyelle McSweeney, Oni Buchanan, Bruce Lack, Dee Airea Matthews, Jeremiah Childers, Marcelo Hernandez Castillo, Derrick Austin, Kathleen Braun & so many others. Without your feedback & loving encouragement this book would not be possible.

Also, mad props to Druvi Acharya for allowing her stunning painting to be used as the cover art for this collection. Find her online at dhruvi. com.

Love & gratitude to the friends & family who put wind in my sails, time after time, in so many ways: Mary Phan, Chanh Phan, Huy Phan, Le Tuan, Bryce Bolton, Sabrina Sideris, Sarah Levine, Danielle Levine, Brian Michael, Matt DeCausin & Ellie "Homegirl" Haberl (my writing buddy, next to whom many of the early drafts of these poems were written in Boulder's sun-drenched coffee shops & along creeks & alongside lazy dogs).

Thank you, Thich Nhat Hanh, for my one true home. To the grocery store workers who risk their lives to put oat milk & salted peanuts & wild orange tea on the shelves. To my 2 good eyes & 1 good heart. To the transportation maintenance workers who repair holes in the earth. Thank you, nurses, for your risk. & To you, lungs, for the crest of each breath. Thank you, violinists, for my soul-bird fire. & To all the forces known & unknown that make living bearable. To every slithering, crawling creature. Thank you, ancestors, for your visions. Gardens of healing & soul-reparations. For every fork & tangent that brought me into being.

This book is set in the typeface Georgia
by The Center for Literary Publishing
at Colorado State University.

Copyediting by Jess Turner.
Proofreading by JV Genova.
Book design and typesetting by Jordan Osborne.
Cover design by Esther Hayes.
Cover art by Dhruvi Acharya:
"under," 66 x 44 inches,
synthetic polymer paint on unprimed linen, 2019.
Printing by Books International.